This
DINOSAUR CODING BOOK
belongs to:

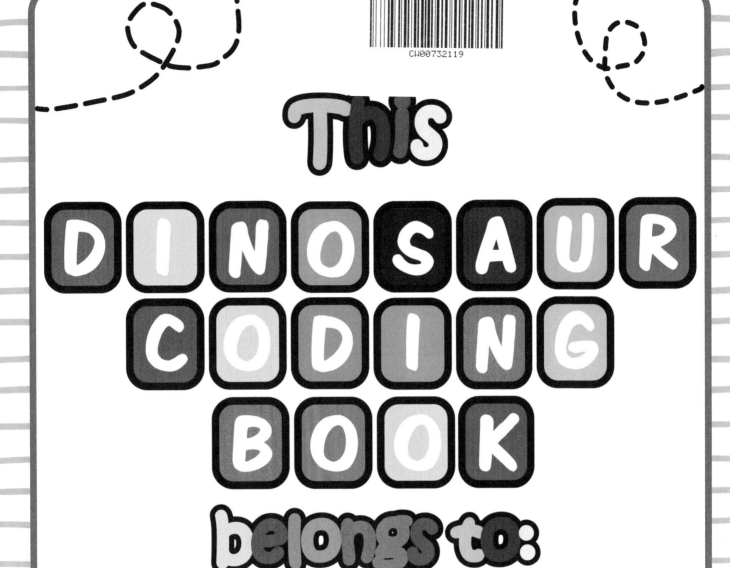

_____

Julia Dream

Table of Contents:

PART 1

Meet Us!

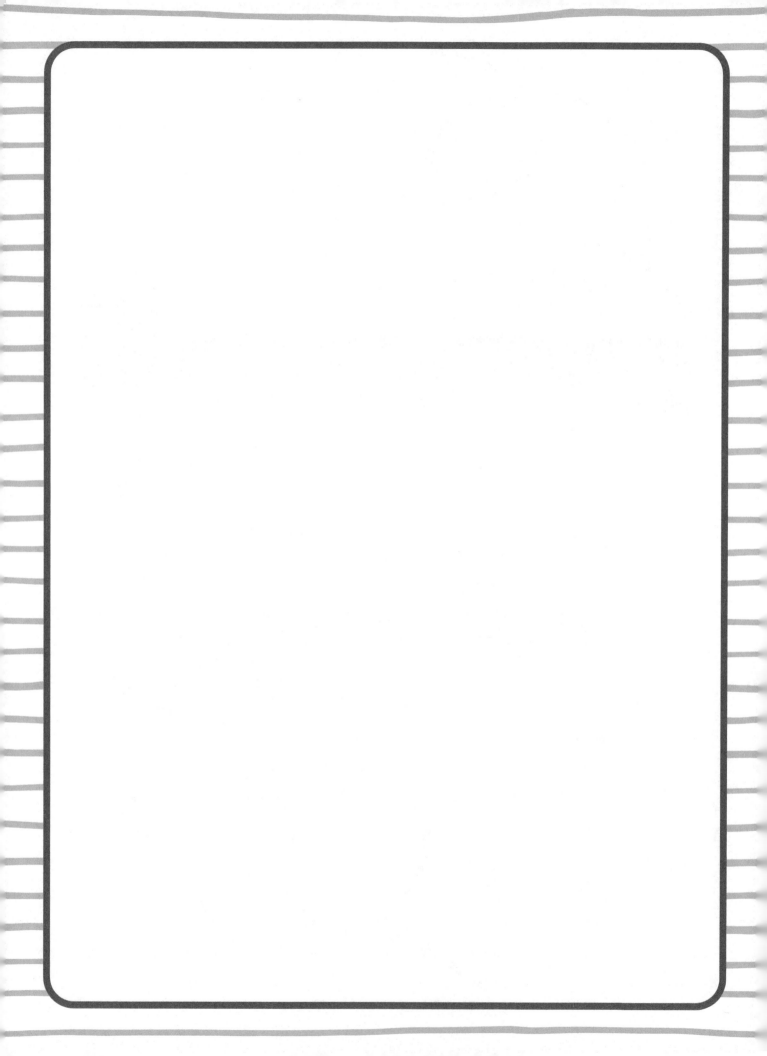

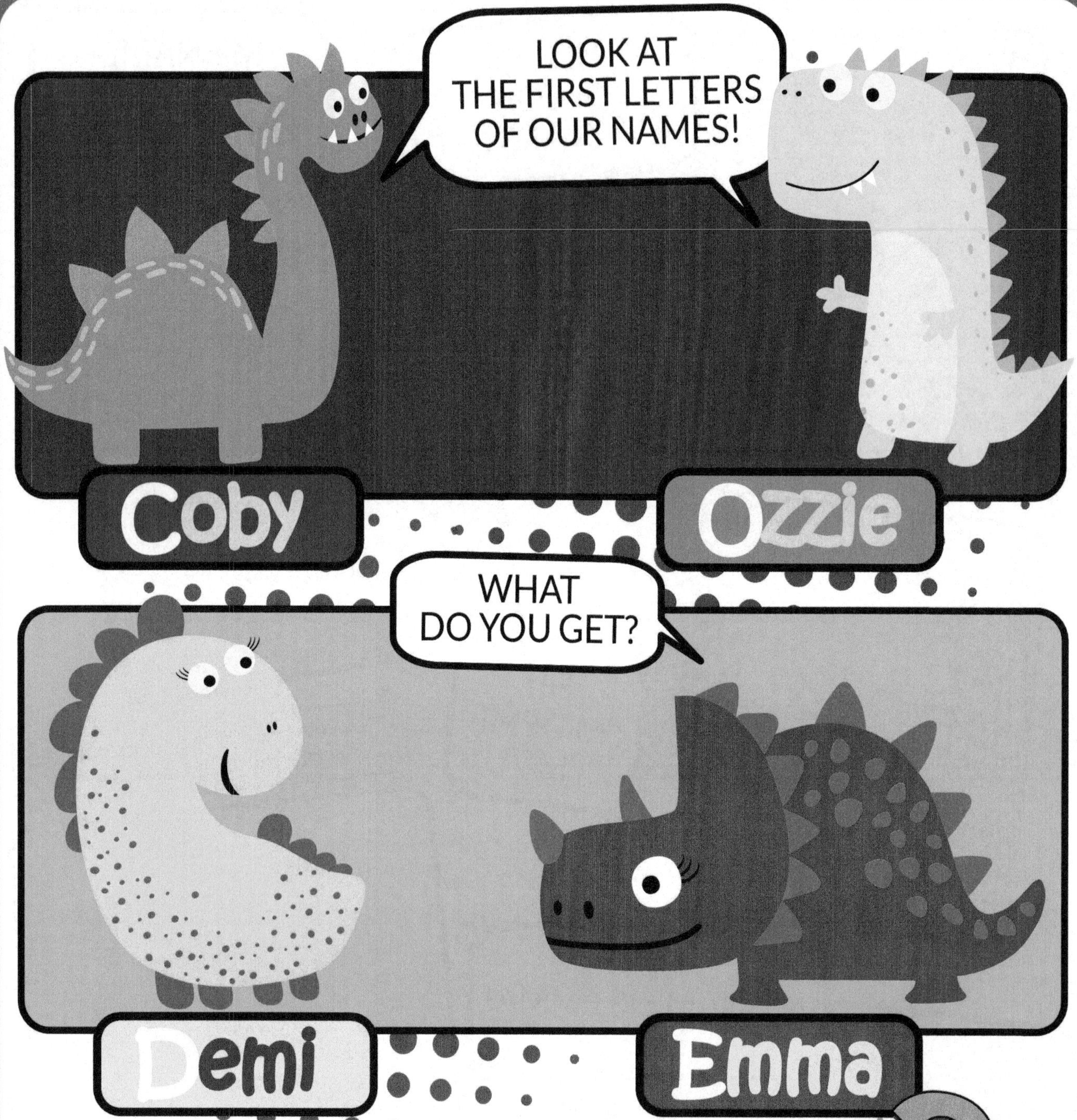

Write the answer in this box.

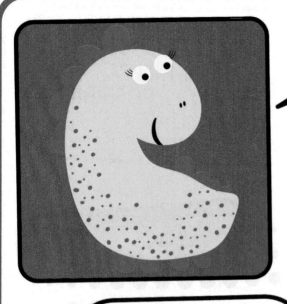

BUT FIRST, LET'S DO SOME ART ACTIVITIES BEFORE WE START CODING.

THANKS TO THESE ACTIVITIES YOU WILL GET TO KNOW US BETTER!

WE HOPE YOU WILL LIKE THEM!

Color the sign.

10

ACTIVITY 1

Meet the Dinosaur, Coby and color the picture!

Meet Us!

Coby is crazy about playing chess and coding!
In his free time, he often goes rollerblading.
His favorite color is dark blue. He has a pet.
It is a goldfish! His name is Finny!

Meet the Dinosaur, Ozzie and color the picture!

Meet Us!

Ozzie loves playing the electric guitar and coding. In his free time, he usually plays computer games. Green is his favorite color and he has a green Snake. Her name is Roxie!

ACTIVITY 3

Meet the Dinosaur, Demi and color the picture!

Demi likes reading comic books and coding.
In her free time, she plays volleyball with her friends.
Her favorite color is pink. Demi doesn't have a pet
but she often helps in a local animal shelter.

ACTIVITY 4

Meet Us!

Emma is a big fan of art. She loves drawing and painting. Of course, she is crazy about coding. In her free time, she listens to pop music. She likes yellow and blue colors. She has a dog. It is a bichon frise. Her name is Coco!

ACTIVITY 5

The Dinosaurs want to meet you! DRAW or WRITE the answers to their questions!

Meet Us!

WHAT ARE YOU CRAZY ABOUT?

WHAT IS YOUR FAVORITE COLOR?

WHAT DO YOU DO IN YOUR FREE TIME?

DO YOU HAVE A PET? IF NOT, WHAT IS YOUR FAVORITE TOY?

How well do you know us?

1 WHO HAS A DOG?

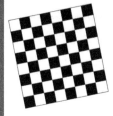

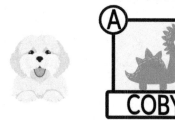 Ⓐ COBY  Ⓑ OZZIE  Ⓒ DEMI  Ⓓ EMMA

2 WHO LOVES PLAYING CHESS?

 Ⓐ COBY  Ⓑ OZZIE  Ⓒ DEMI  Ⓓ EMMA

3 WHO PLAYS VOLLEYBALL?

 Ⓐ COBY  Ⓑ OZZIE  Ⓒ DEMI  Ⓓ EMMA

4 WHO HAS A SNAKE?

 Ⓐ COBY  Ⓑ OZZIE  Ⓒ DEMI  Ⓓ EMMA

5 WHO LOVES LISTENING TO POP MUSIC?

 Ⓐ COBY  Ⓑ OZZIE  Ⓒ DEMI  Ⓓ EMMA

6 WHO IS CRAZY ABOUT ART?

A  COBY

B  OZZIE

C  DEMI

D  EMMA

7 WHO PLAYS THE ELECTRIC GUITAR?

A  COBY

B  OZZIE

C  DEMI

D  EMMA

8 WHO HELPS IN A LOCAL ANIMAL SHELTER?

A  COBY

B  OZZIE

C  DEMI

D  EMMA

9 WHAT IS THE NAME OF COBY'S GOLDFISH?

A  NEMO

B  FINLEY

C  FINNY

D  BUBBA

10 WHAT IS THE NAME OF A CUTE BICHON FRISE?

A  LUNA

B  COCO

C  CLEO

D  ZOE

17

11 WHO OFTEN GOES ROLLERBLADING?

A  COBY B  OZZIE C  DEMI D  EMMA

12 WHO LIKES COMIC BOOKS?

A  COBY B  OZZIE C  DEMI D  EMMA

13 WHOSE FAVORITE COLOR IS GREEN?

A  COBY B  OZZIE C  DEMI D  EMMA

14 WHO DOES NOT HAVE A PET?

A  COBY B  OZZIE C  DEMI D  EMMA

15 WHO LIKES DARK BLUE COLOR?

A  COBY B  OZZIE C  DEMI D  EMMA

ACTIVITY 6

Become your favorite dinosaur by cutting out this paper facemask!

Instructions:
1. Cut out a facemask and straps on the dotted lines.
2. Attach straps with glue or tape for the best-desired fit.
3. Use your imagination to play!

Coby

Coby

Coby

ACTIVITY 7

Become your favorite dinosaur by cutting out this paper facemask!

Instructions:
1. Cut out a facemask and straps on the dotted lines.
2. Attach straps with glue or tape for the best-desired fit.
3. Use your imagination to play!

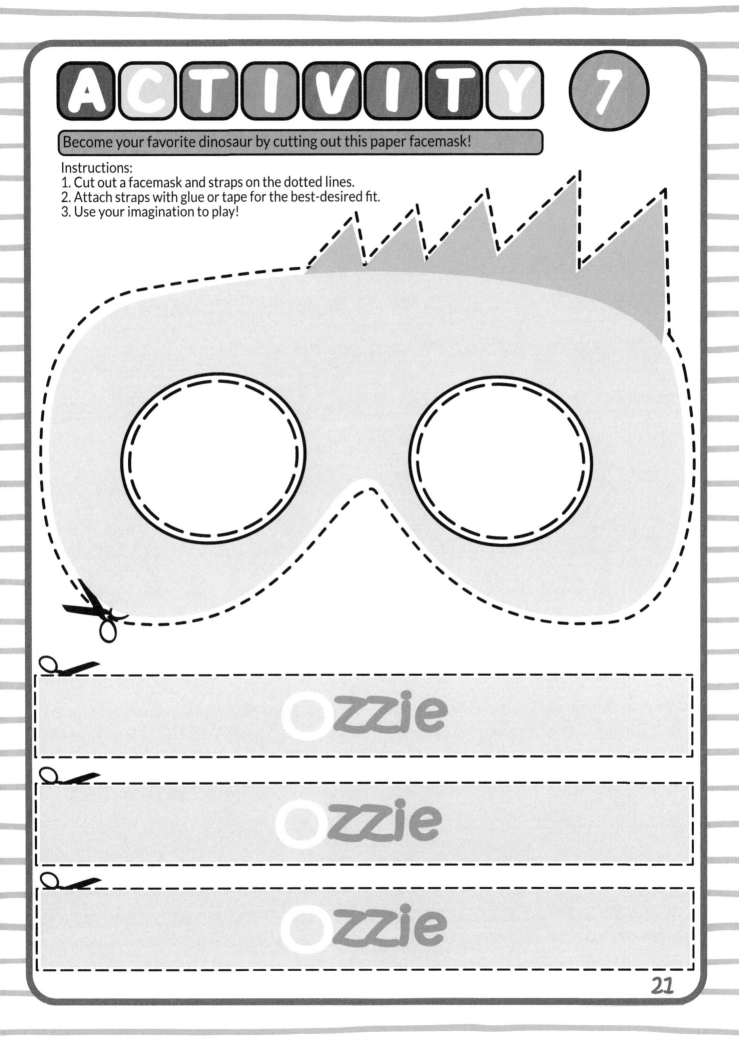

Ozzie

Ozzie

Ozzie

ACTIVITY

Become your favorite dinosaur by cutting out this paper facemask!

Instructions:
1. Cut out a facemask and straps on the dotted lines.
2. Attach straps with glue or tape for the best-desired fit.
3. Use your imagination to play!

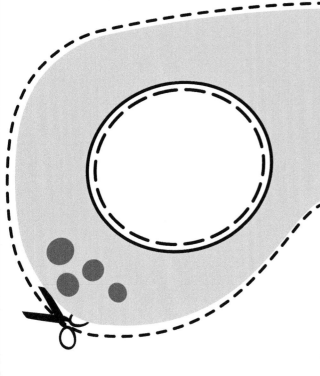
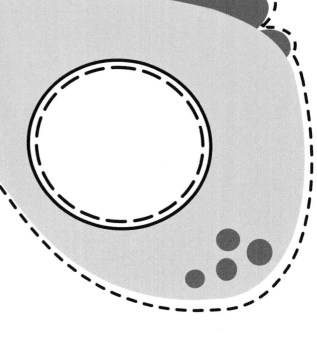

Demi

Demi

Demi

ACTIVITY

Become your favorite dinosaur by cutting out this paper facemask!

Instructions:
1. Cut out a facemask and straps on the dotted lines.
2. Attach straps with glue or tape for the best-desired fit.
3. Use your imagination to play!

Emma

Emma

Emma

PART 2
Let's Code!

Step 1
Coding Warm-Up

Sequence. Put the pictures in the correct order.

  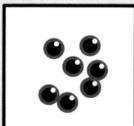 

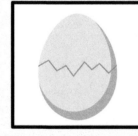   

30

Sequence. Put the pictures in the correct order.

Pattern recognition. Complete the patterns.

CODE OUR FRIENDLY CATERPILLAR BY REPEATING THE PATTERNS!

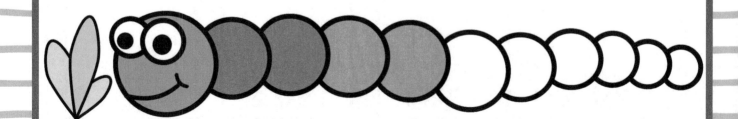

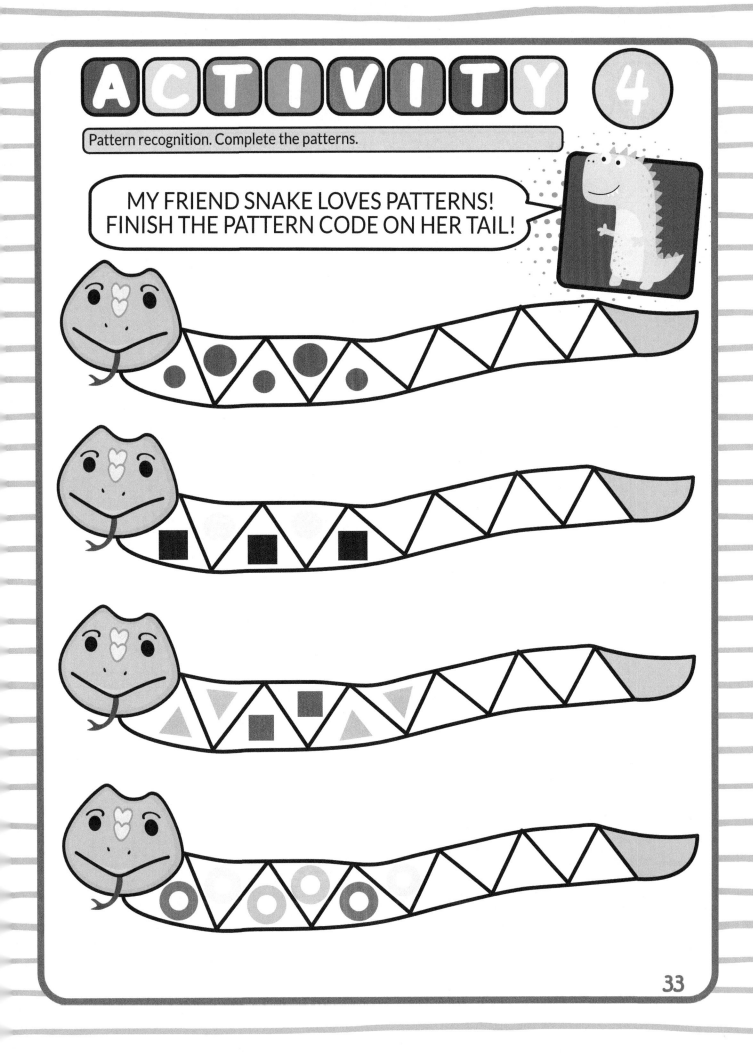

ACTIVITY 5

Debugging. What's wrong with this picture. Circle 8 things that shouldn't be there.

LET'S GO ON A SAFARI TRIP!

ACTIVITY 6

Debugging. What's wrong with this picture. Circle 8 things that shouldn't be there.

ACTIVITY

Decomposition. Count the animals.

 _____

 _____

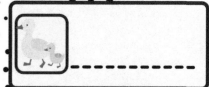 _____

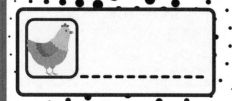 _____

 _____

 _____

ACTIVITY 8

Decomposition. Count the shapes.

DON'T COUNT WHISKERS AND MOUTHS. I'VE DRAWN THEM :)

CIRCLES _____

SQUARES _____

TRIANGLES _____

RECTANGLES _____

ACTIVITY 9

Abstraction. Circle the things you do NOT need for school.

HINT!
THERE ARE 8 THINGS
YOU HAVE TO
CIRCLE!

38

ACTIVITY 10

Abstraction. Circle the things you do NOT need for a mountain trip.

AS I SEE YOU NEED TO CIRCLE 8 THINGS!

Loops. Write HOW MANY LOOPS are required for each activity below.

LOOP IS A SET OF ACTIONS THAT YOU OR A COMPUTER NEED TO REPEAT TO COMPLETE A TASK!

How many puddles does Coby need to jump over?

How many baskets does Emma need to score?

How many pairs of dirty shoes does Demi need to clean?

How many car toys does Ozzie need do pack?

40

ACTIVITY 12

Loops. Write HOW MANY LOOPS are required for each activity below.

HELP BABIES REACH THEIR PARENTS.
COUNT HOW MANY FLOWERS OR LEAVES
DO THEY NEED TO JUMP ON TO GET
TO THEIR BELOVED PARENTS.

41

Branching. Match an IF/THEN statement by drawing a line to connect two pictures.

 If you are cold ......

than you get pink.

 If it rains ......

than go to bed.

 If you mix red and white ......

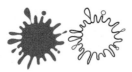

than put on a sweater.

 If you are sleepy ......

than take an umbrella.

ACTIVITY 14

Branching. Match an IF/THEN statement by drawing a line to connect two pictures.

1 If you see a red traffic light ......

than drink a lot of water.

2 If you are thirsty ......

than call the fire brigade.

3 If you see fire ......

than give a hug.

4 If someone is sad ......

than you must stop.

Color the balloon according to the color code.

CODE

Color the balloon according to your **OWN** color code.

CODE

45

Draw the other half.

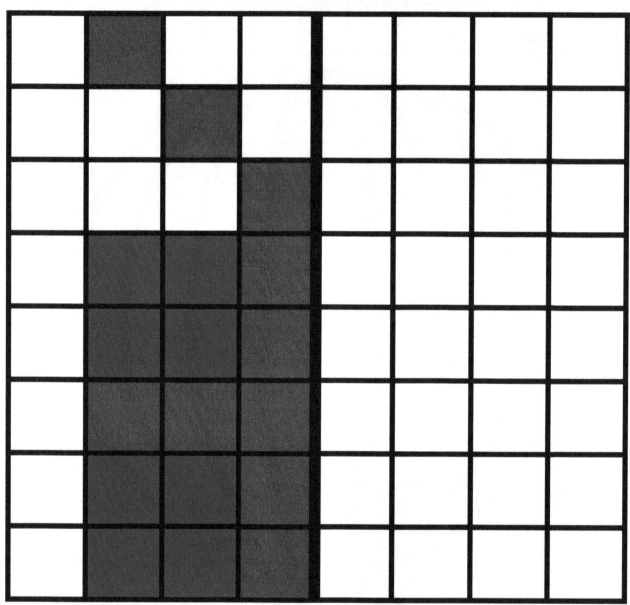

I LOVE GETTING GIFTS!
BUT THIS GIFT IS NOT READY.
FINISH THE OTHER SIDE
OF THE PICTURE BY FOLLOWING
THE COLOR CODE.

ACTIVITY 18

Draw the other half.

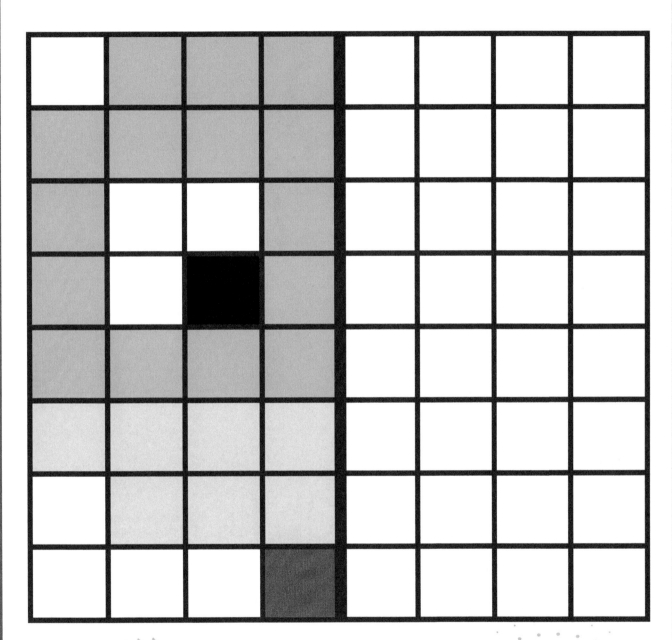

DO YOU REMEMBER MY FRIEND SNAKE? HER NAME IS ROXIE! COLOR HER OTHER HALF BY THE COLOR CODE!

We are going on a school trip. Use the code to find out where we are sitting.

BUS DRIVER

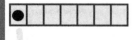  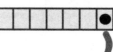 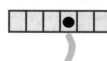 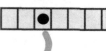

SCHOOL BUS

THERE ARE TWO FREE SEATS.
TAKE YOUR FRIEND
AND GO WITH US!
DRAW YOUR FACES IN
EMPTY WINDOWS!

48

Fill in the table with the proper drawings using the given code.

CODE →	↑	↑	↑	↑
♥	♥			
■		■		
✿			✿	

PAY ATTENTION TO THE SIZE! TRY TO DRAW THINGS BIGGER AND BIGGER!

49

ACTIVITY 21

Sudoku.

REMEMBER! IN SUDOKU PUZZLES THE ELEMENTS MUST APPEAR ONLY ONCE IN EACH

ROW , COLUMN , AND BLOCK .

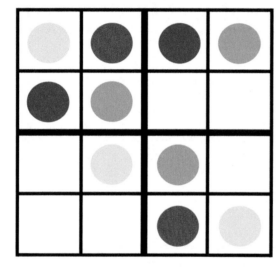

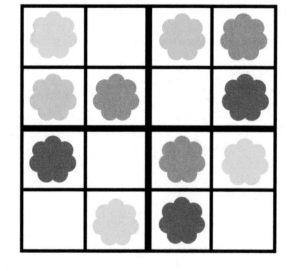

DRAW THE MISSING SHAPES!

ACTIVITY 20

Sudoku.

1

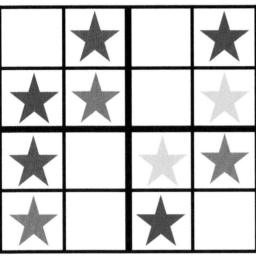

2

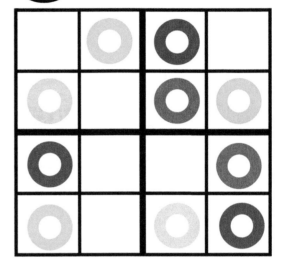

3

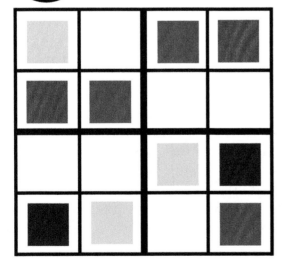

4

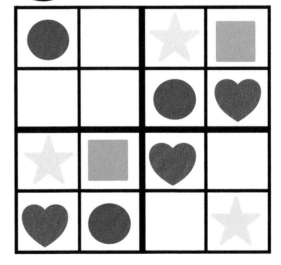

CERTIFICATE of COMPLETION

This certificate is awarded to

....

for successful completion of

THE FIRST STEP IN CODING

„CODING WARM-UP"

Step 2

Arrows, Directions and Coding

ACTIVITY 1

Sequence. Help our friendly Dinosaurs to get to their destinations. Draw the missing arrows.

You can use: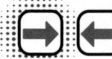

1

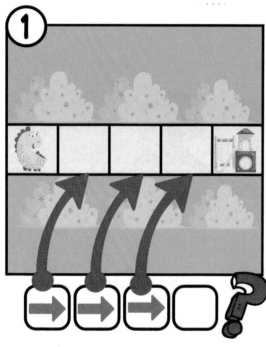

2

3

4

Sequence. Draw the missing arrows to help our friends to get to the beach.

You can use:

①

②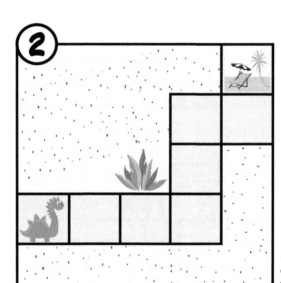

③

 WAIT FOR ME!

ACTIVITY 3

Sequence. Draw the arrow code to help our friends to get to the playground.

You can use:

ACTIVITY 4

Sequence. Draw the arrow code to help our friends to get to the playground.

You can use:

1

2

Sequence. Draw the arrow code to help our friends to get to the ZOO.

You can use:

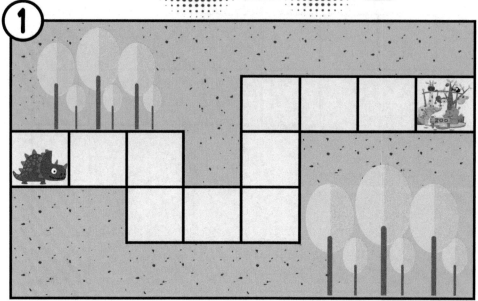

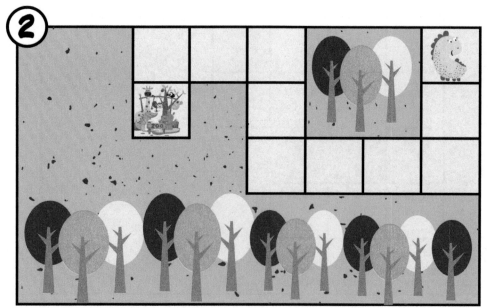

ACTIVITY 6

Sequence. Draw the arrow code to help our friends to get to the ZOO.

You can use:

1

2

ACTIVITY 7

Debugging. Find the incorrect command in the arrow code and circle it.

LOOK AT THE EXAMPLE!

①

②

LET'S GO BUG HUNTING!

ACTIVITY 8

Debugging. Find the incorrect command in the arrow code and circle it.

HINT: there are 2 „BUGS" in each code!

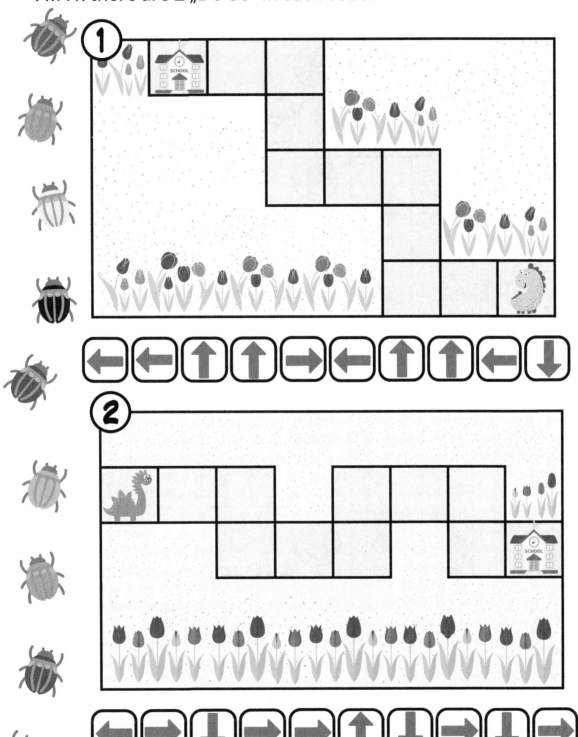

ACTIVITY

Debugging. Choose the correct code: A or B.

1

A ↑ → ↑ → → ↑ ↑

B ↑ → ↑ → → ↓ ↓

THE CORRECT ANSWER IS: ◯

2

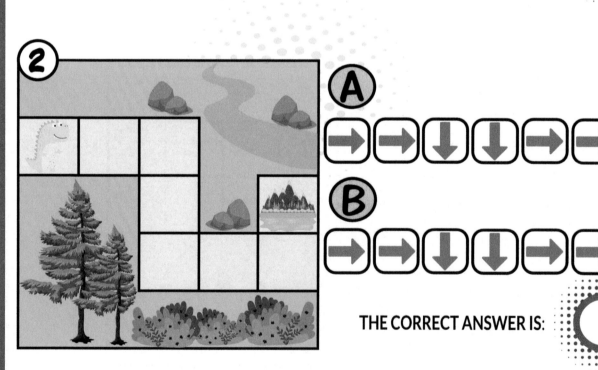

A → → ↓ ↓ → → ↓

B → → ↓ ↓ → → ↑

THE CORRECT ANSWER IS: ◯

ACTIVITY 10

Debugging. Choose the correct code: A or B.

1

A ➡️ ⬆️ ⬆️ ➡️ ➡️ ⬇️ ⬇️ ➡️ ➡️ ➡️

B ➡️ ⬆️ ⬆️ ⬆️ ➡️ ➡️ ⬆️ ⬆️ ➡️ ➡️ ➡️

2

A ⬅️ ⬇️ ⬇️ ⬅️ ⬅️ ⬅️ ⬇️ ⬅️ ⬅️ ⬅️

B ⬅️ ⬇️ ⬇️ ⬅️ ⬅️ ⬇️ ⬇️ ⬅️ ⬅️ ⬅️

Go Wild :)

Play, have fun & create your own codes for our friends!
Plan your own route and a finish line.

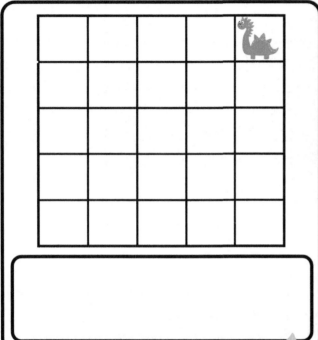

That is a place for your arrow code.

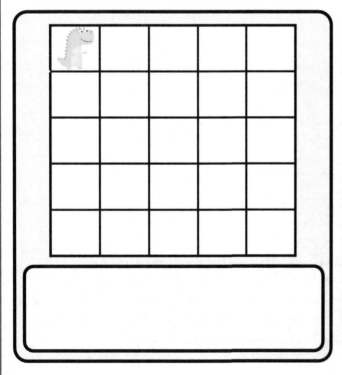

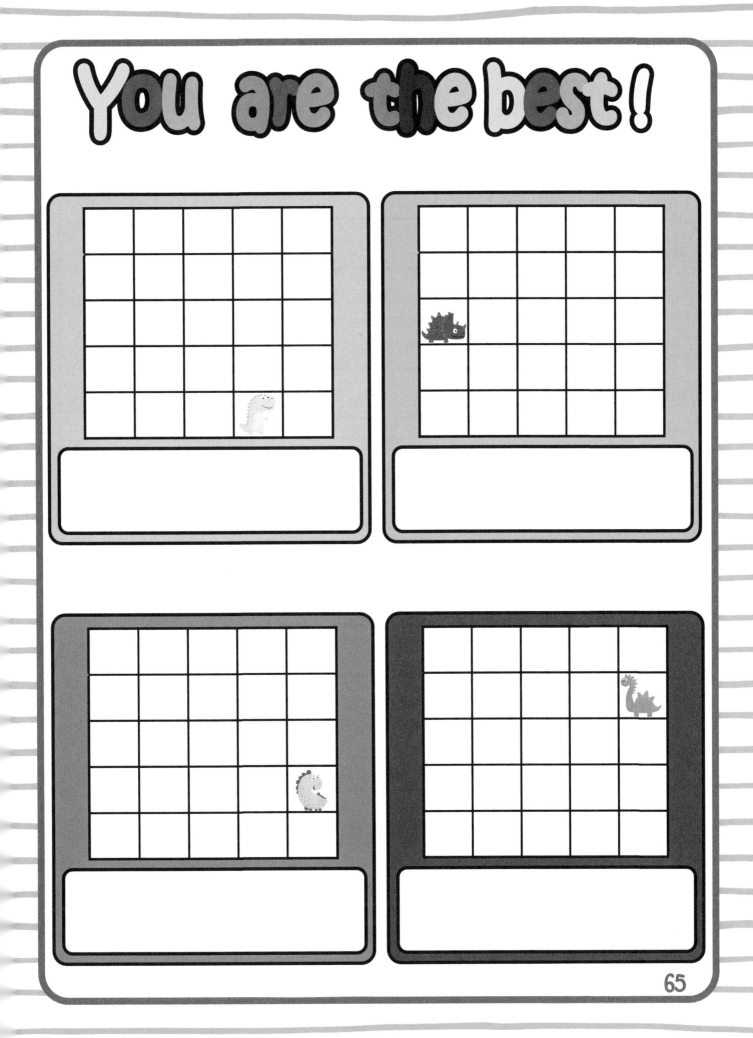

You are gifted!

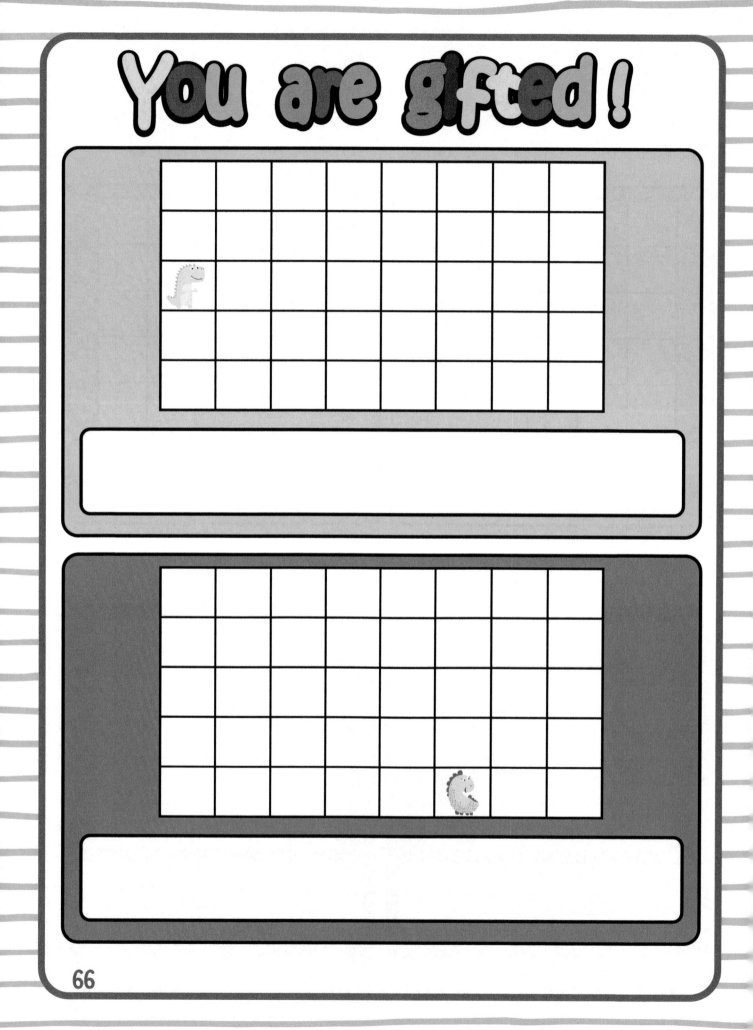

You are creative!

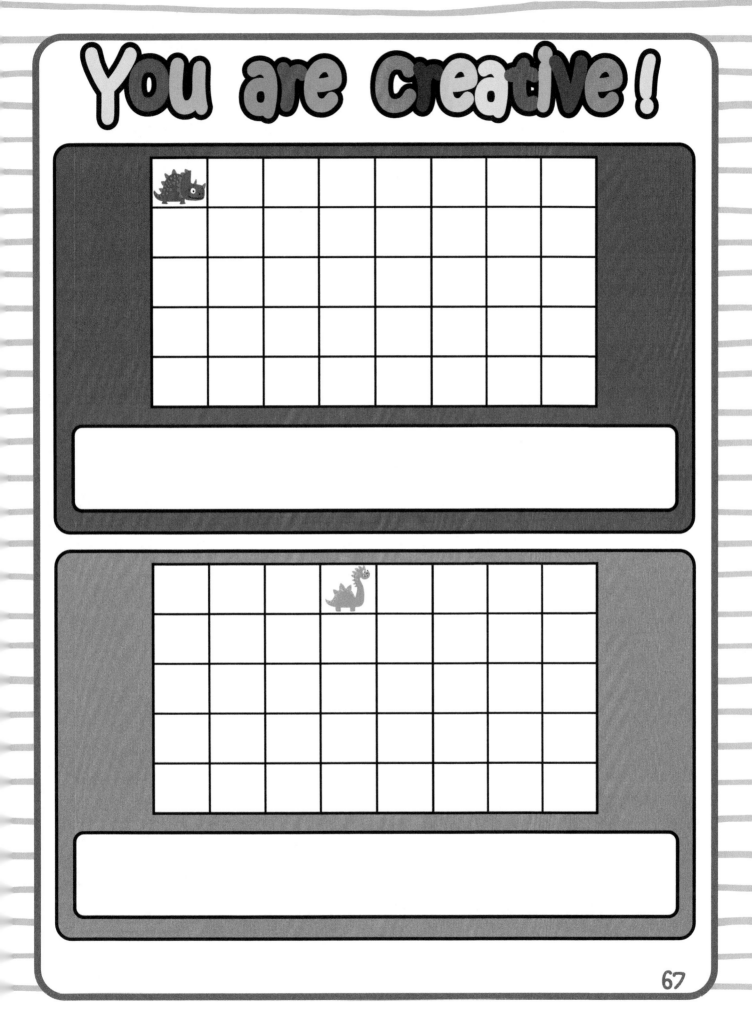

Loops!

IT'S TIME WE PRACTISED LOOPS!

LOOPS ARE THINGS OR ACTIONS THAT REPEAT MULTIPLE TIMES!

LOOK AT THESE EXAMPLES:

example 1:
Ozzie to get to the playground has to move forward 4 times. We can write an arrow code for this action. It is easy! We can also write a shorter code using a LOOP!

example 2:
Ozzie to get to the pet shop needs to move forward and then go up. He has to repeat this action 3 times. The arrow code has 6 blocks,
But the code with LOOPS has only two blocks!

example 1:

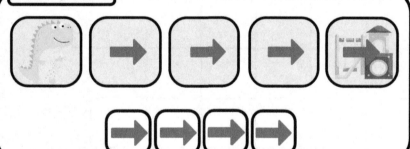

LOOP

REPEAT 4

THIS ARROW CODE HAS 4 BLOCKS

THE CODE WITH A LOOP HAS ONLY 1 BLOCK!

example 2:

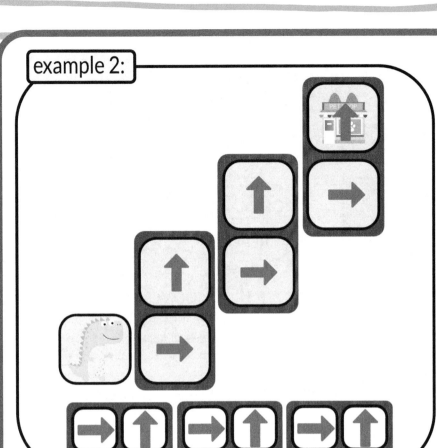

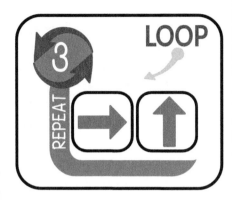

LOOP

HAVE A CLOSER LOOK AT OUR LOOPS!

Write the number of loops
(repeated actions) here.

example 1:

example 2:

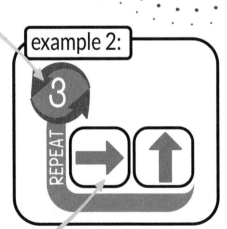

Draw the arrow code / action
which is repeated here.

Loops. Look at the pictures and choose the correct code.

1

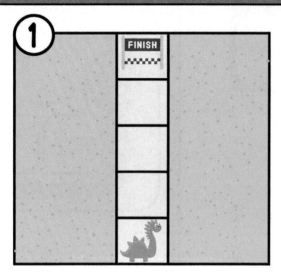

HOW MANY TIMES IS THE MOVE REPEATED?

WHAT KIND OF MOVE IS REPEATED?

 **A**

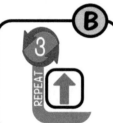 **B**

 **C**

THE CORRECT ANSWER IS:

2

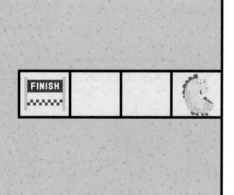

 **A**

 **B**

 **C**

THE CORRECT ANSWER IS:

ACTIVITY 12

Loops. Look at the pictures and choose the correct code.

1

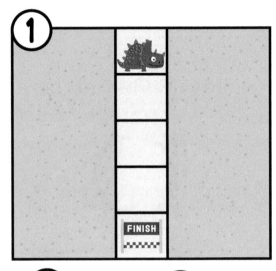

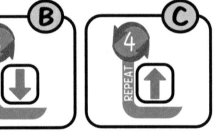

THE CORRECT ANSWER IS:

2

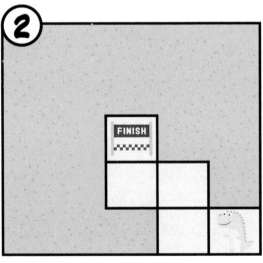

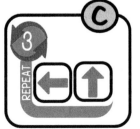

THE CORRECT ANSWER IS:

ACTIVITY 13

Loops. Look at the pictures and choose the correct code.

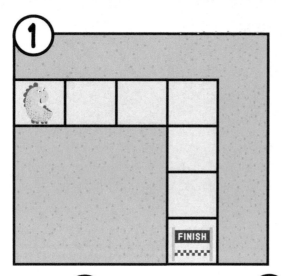

1

THE CORRECT ANSWER IS:

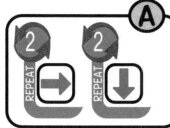

A

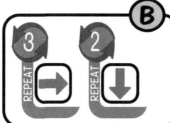

B

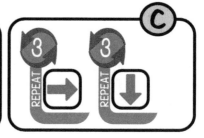

C

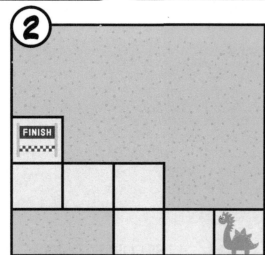

2

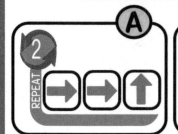

A

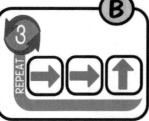

B

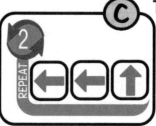

C

THE CORRECT ANSWER IS:

72

Loops. Look at the pictures and choose the correct code.

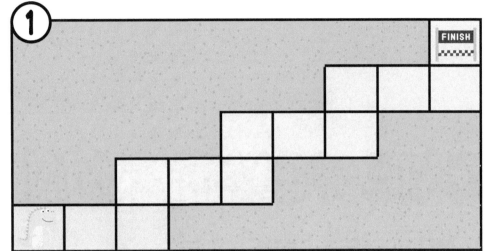

1

FINISH

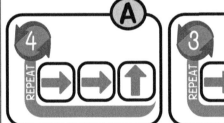

A

REPEAT 4 ➡️ ➡️ ⬆️

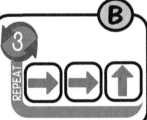

B

REPEAT 3 ➡️ ➡️ ⬆️

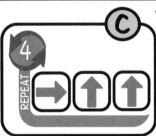

C

REPEAT 4 ➡️ ⬆️ ⬆️

THE CORRECT ANSWER IS:

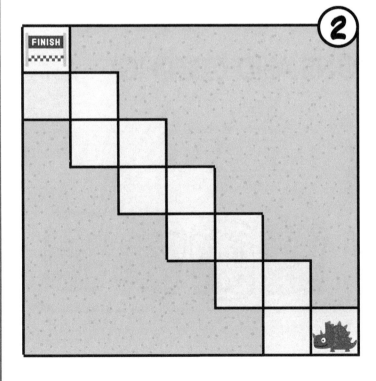

2

FINISH

A

REPEAT 5 ⬅️ ⬆️

THE CORRECT ANSWER IS:

B

REPEAT 6 ⬅️ ⬆️

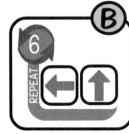

C

REPEAT 6 ➡️ ⬆️

73

CERTIFICATE of COMPLETION

This certificate is awarded to

....

for successful completion of

THE SECOND STEP IN CODING

„ARROWS, DIRECTIONS AND CODING"

GOOD JOB!

Step 3

Coordinates and Coding

Coordinates!

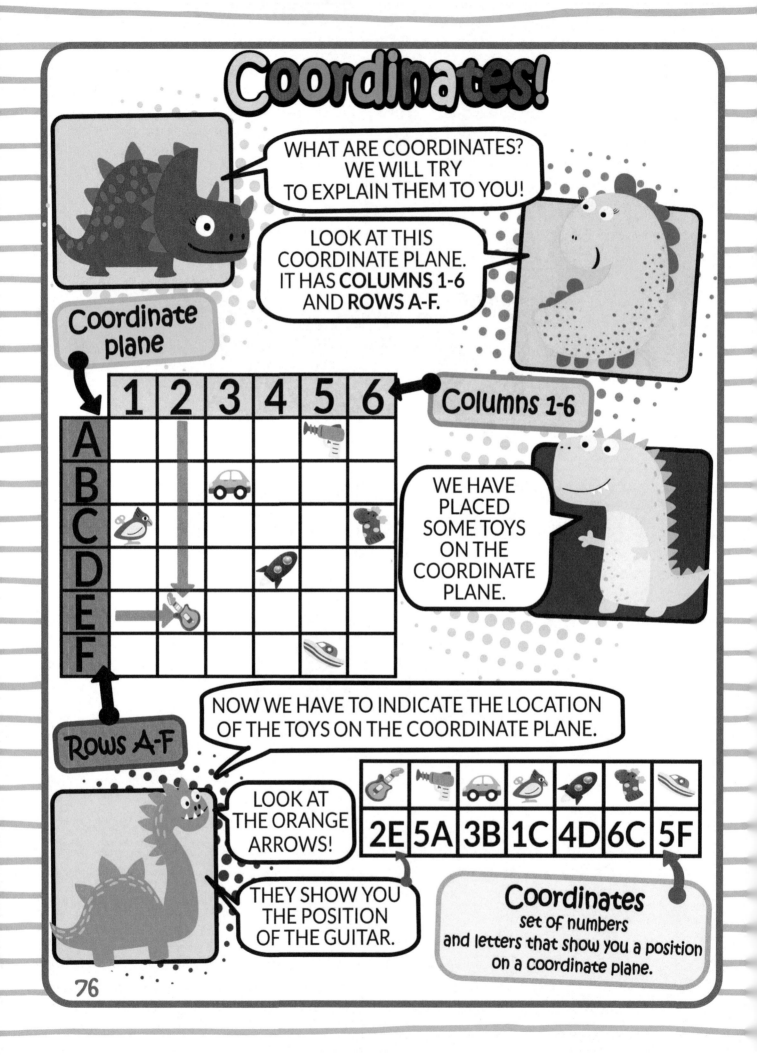

WHAT ARE COORDINATES? WE WILL TRY TO EXPLAIN THEM TO YOU!

LOOK AT THIS COORDINATE PLANE. IT HAS **COLUMNS 1-6** AND **ROWS A-F**.

Coordinate plane

Columns 1-6

WE HAVE PLACED SOME TOYS ON THE COORDINATE PLANE.

Rows A-F

NOW WE HAVE TO INDICATE THE LOCATION OF THE TOYS ON THE COORDINATE PLANE.

LOOK AT THE ORANGE ARROWS!

THEY SHOW YOU THE POSITION OF THE GUITAR.

2E	5A	3B	1C	4D	6C	5F

Coordinates
set of numbers and letters that show you a position on a coordinate plane.

76

ACTIVITY ①

Where are the monsters? Choose the correct answer A or B.

	1	2	3	4	5	6
A						🦖
B		🦕				
C						
D	🦖			🦕		
E		🦕				
F						🦕

IS IT A or B? WRITE THE CORRECT ANSWER!

① Ⓐ 4B Ⓑ 2E ◯

② Ⓐ 6F Ⓑ 1D ◯

③ Ⓐ 1D Ⓑ 4E ◯

④ Ⓐ 2A Ⓑ 2B ◯

⑤ Ⓐ 4D Ⓑ 5C ◯

⑥ Ⓐ 3C Ⓑ 6A ◯

ACTIVITY 2

Match the coordinates with the correct piece of the picture.

	1	2	3	4	5	6	7
A							
B							
C							
D							
E							
F							
G							

4B   6D

3A   5F

6F   6A

3D   3E

ACTIVITY 3

Match the coordinates with the correct piece of the picture.

	1	2	3	4	5	6	7
A							
B							
C							
D							
E							
F							
G							

6B

1G

2D

1C

7G

3B

3F

5E

79

Color the circles according to the code on the coordinate board.

	1	2	3	4
A	⚪	⚪	⚫	⚪
B	⚫	⚫	⚫	⚫
C	⚫	⚫	⚫	⚫
D	⚫	⚫	⚫	⚪

4A   2C   3D   1B   4D

2D   3C   1A   4B   1C

ACTIVITY 5

In empty boxes draw and color the shapes according to code on the coordinate board.

	1	2	3	4
A	■	▲	♥	◆
B	▼		◉	■
C	◉	◆	●	▼
D		★	▲	★

3A
4D
1C
2A
3B

1A
3C
4C
2B
1B

ACTIVITY 6

Use the code to color the coordinate board and reveal the picture.

	1	2	3	4	5	6	7	8	9	10
A										
B										
C										
D										
E										
F										
G										
H										
I										

You need:

1E, 1F, 2D, 2F, 2G, 3C, 3D, 3E, 3F, 3G, 4H, 4I, 5H, 5I, 6H, 7H, 8H, 8I, 9H, 9I, 10G.

4D, 4E, 4F, 4G, 5C, 5D, 5E, 5F, 5G, 6B, 6C, 6D, 6E, 6F, 6G, 7B, 7C, 7D, 7E, 7F, 7G, 8C, 8D, 8E, 8F, 8G, 9D, 9E, 9F, 9G.

2E :)

ACTIVITY

Use the code to color the coordinate board and reveal the picture.

	1	2	3	4	5	6	7	8	9	10
A										
B										
C										
D										
E										
F										
G										
H										
I										

You need: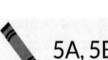

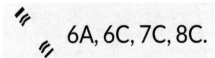 5A, 5B, 5C, 5D, 5E.

6B, 7B, 6D, 7D, 8D, 9D.

 1I, 2I, 3I, 4I, 5I, 6I 7I, 8I, 9I, 10I.

1F, 2F, 2G, 3F, 3G, 3H, 4F, 4G, 4H, 5F, 5G, 5H, 6F, 6G, 6H, 7F, 7G, 7H, 8F, 8G, 8H, 9F, 9G, 10F.

 6A, 6C, 7C, 8C.

ACTIVITY  8

Emma wants to visit her friend Coby. Use the coordinate code to find out which way she goes. Color the squares on the coordinate board in blue.

	1	2	3	4	5	6	7	8
A								
B								
C								
D								
E								
F								
G								
H								

1C 2C 3C 4C 4D 4E 4F 5F 6F 7F 7G 7H 8H

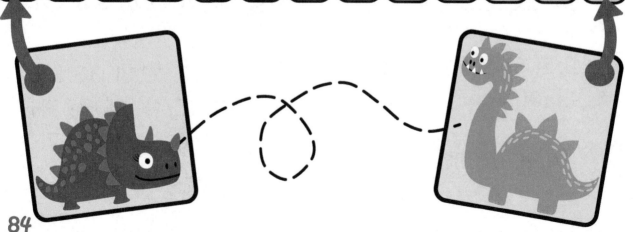

84

ACTIVITY 9

Demi wants to visit her friend Ozzie. Use the coordinate code to find out which way she goes. Color the squares on the coordinate board in yellow.

	1	2	3	4	5	6	7	8
A								
B								
C								
D								
E								
F								
G								
H								

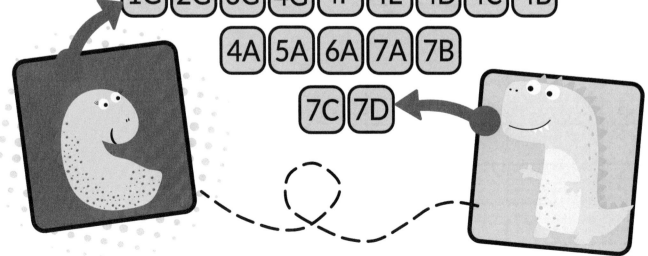

1G 2G 3G 4G 4F 4E 4D 4C 4B

4A 5A 6A 7A 7B

7C 7D

ACTIVITY

Debugging. Find the incorrect command in the code and circle it.

LOOK AT THE EXAMPLE!

	1	2	3
A			
B			
C			

3A 3B (2A) 2C 1C

---

①

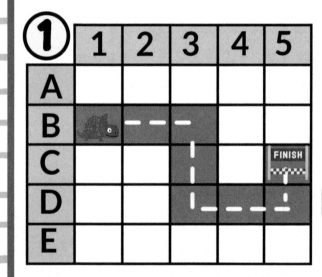

	1	2	3	4	5
A					
B					
C					FINISH
D					
E					

1B 2B 3B 3C 3D 3E 5D 5C

---

②

	1	2	3	4	5
A				FINISH	
B					
C					
D					
E					

1E 1D 1C 1B 2B 2A 3B 4A

Debugging. Find the incorrect command in the code and circle it.

HINT: there are 2 „BUGS" in each code!

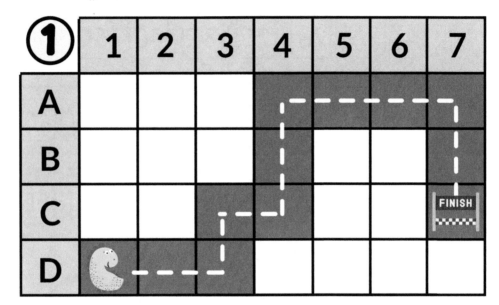

①
1D 2D 3D 4D 4C 4B 4A 5A 6A 7A 7B 6B

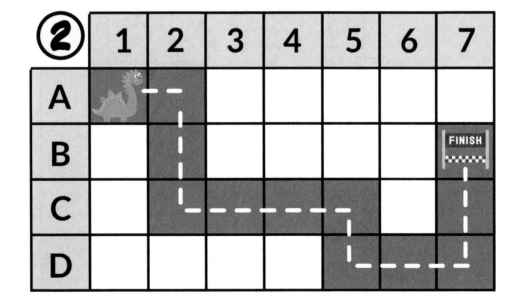

②
1B 2A 2B 2C 3C 4C 5C 6C 6D 7D 7C 7B

87

Coby wants to get to the playground. Which coordinate code is correct A, B or C?

A — 1A — 2A — 2B — 2C — 3C — 4C — 5C — 5D — 5E —

B — 1A — 2A — 3A — 4A — 5A — 5B — 4B — 4C — 5C

C — 1A — 2A — 3A — 3B — 3C — 3D — 4D — 5D — 5E —

THE CORRECT ANSWER IS:

	1	2	3	4	5
A					
B					
C					
D					
E					

ACTIVITY 13

Get Emma, Demi and, Ozzie to their destinations. Which code is correct A or B?

1

	1	2	3	4	5
A					
B					
C					
D					
E					

A --1D- 2D- 3D- 3C- 3B- 3A- 4A- 5A--

B --1D- 2D- 3D- 3C- 3B- 4B- 5B- 5A--

THE CORRECT ANSWER IS:

2

	1	2	3	4	5
A					
B					
C					
D					
E					

A 5D- 4D- 3D- 3C- 2C- 2B- 2A- 1A- 1B

B 5D- 4D- 3D- 3C- 3B- 3A- 2A- 1A- 1B

THE CORRECT ANSWER IS:

3

	1	2	3	4	5
A					
B					
C					
D					
E					

A --2E- 2D- 2C- 3C- 3D- 4D- 5D- 5C--

B --2E- 2D- 2C- 2B- 3B- 4B- 4C- 5C--

THE CORRECT ANSWER IS:

Go Wild :)

Play, have fun & create your own codes with coordinates for our friends!

The place for your code.
Start from this coordinate!
Draw your own route
and a finish line / destination place.

	1	2	3	4	5
A					
B					
C					
D					
E					

5A,

	1	2	3	4	5
A					
B					
C					
D					
E					

1B,

You are amazing !

	1	2	3	4	5
A					
B					
C					
D					
E					

3E,

	1	2	3	4	5
A					
B					
C					
D					
E					

1E,

You are a great kid !

	1	2	3	4	5	6	7	8
A								
B								
C								
D								
E								
F								
G								
H								

4A,

You are awesome !

	1	2	3	4	5	6	7	8
A								
B								
C								
D								
E								
F								
G								
H								

1G,

CERTIFICATE of COMPLETION

This certificate is awarded to

....

for successful completion of

THE THIRD STEP IN CODING

„COORDINATES AND CODING"

WELL DONE

Step 4

Binary System and Coding

Binary system!

LET'S TALK ABOUT BINARY SYSTEM NOW!

BINARY SYSTEM IS USED IN OUR COMPUTERS!

THIS SYSTEM USES ONLY TWO NUMBERS:

IT IS HARD TO IMAGINE BUT EVERYTHING YOU SEE ON THE COMPUTER SCREEN: LETTERS, NUMBERS, PICTURES IS MADE UP OF A DIFFERENT COMBINATION OF THESE TWO NUMBERS: „0" AND „1"!

LOOK AT SOME LETTERS IN A BINARY CODE!

„A"
01000001

„C"
01000011

„B"
01000010

„D"
01000100

96

Convert the binary codes into images.

0	0	0	1	1	0	0	0
0	0	1	1	1	1	0	0
0	1	1	1	1	1	1	0
1	1	1	1	1	1	1	1
0	1	0	1	1	0	1	0
0	1	1	1	1	1	1	0
0	1	1	0	0	1	1	0
0	1	1	0	0	1	1	0

0	0	0	1	0	0	0	0
0	0	1	1	0	0	0	0
1	1	0	1	0	0	0	0
1	1	1	1	0	0	0	1
0	1	1	1	1	1	1	0
0	1	1	1	1	1	1	0
0	1	1	0	0	1	1	0
0	1	1	0	0	1	1	0

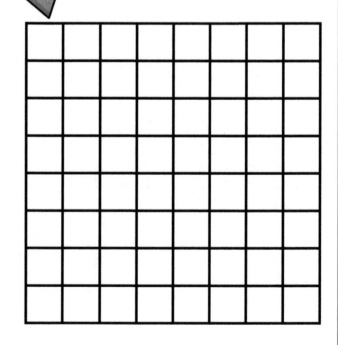

Convert the binary codes into images.

0	0	0	1	1	1	0	0
0	0	1	1	1	1	1	0
1	1	1	1	1	0	1	0
1	1	1	1	1	1	1	0
1	1	1	1	1	0	1	0
1	1	0	1	1	0	1	0
1	1	0	1	1	0	1	1
1	1	0	1	1	0	0	0

0	0	0	1	1	0	0	0
0	0	0	1	1	1	0	0
0	0	0	1	1	1	1	0
0	0	0	1	1	1	1	1
0	0	0	1	0	0	0	0
1	1	1	1	1	1	1	1
0	1	1	1	1	1	1	0
0	0	1	1	1	1	0	0

ACTIVITY 3

Convert the binary code into an image.

0	0	0	1	0	0	0	0
1	1	1	0	0	0	0	0
1	0	1	0	0	0	0	0
1	1	1	0	0	0	0	0
0	0	1	0	0	0	0	0
0	0	1	0	0	0	0	0
0	0	1	0	0	0	0	1
0	0	1	1	1	1	1	0
0	0	1	1	1	1	1	0
0	0	1	1	1	1	1	0
0	0	1	0	0	0	1	0
0	0	1	0	0	0	1	0
0	0	1	0	0	0	1	0
0	0	1	0	0	0	1	0

100

ACTIVITY

Convert the binary code into an image.

0	0	0	0	0	1	0	0	0	0	0	0	0	0
0	0	0	0	0	1	1	1	0	0	0	0	0	1
0	1	1	1	1	1	1	1	1	0	0	0	1	0
1	1	0	1	1	1	1	1	1	1	0	0	1	1
1	1	1	1	1	1	1	1	1	1	1	1	1	1
0	1	1	1	1	1	1	1	1	1	1	1	1	1
0	0	1	1	1	1	1	1	1	1	1	1	1	1
0	0	0	0	0	0	0	0	0	0	0	0	1	1
0	0	0	0	0	0	0	0	0	0	0	0	0	1

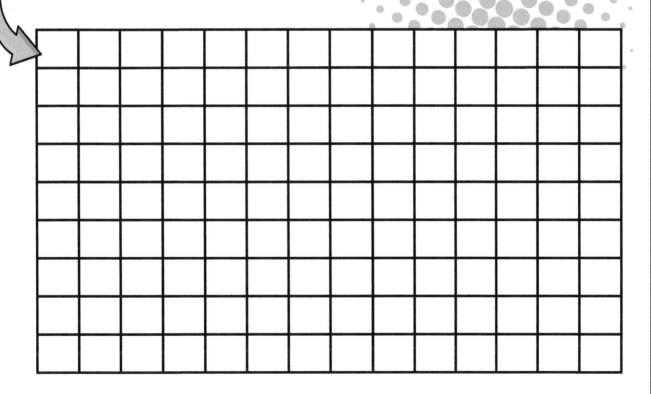

ACTIVITY 6

Convert the images into the binary codes.

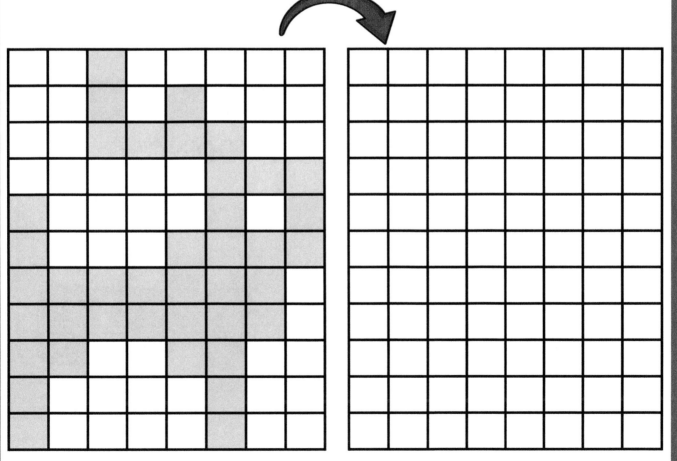

CERTIFICATE of COMPLETION

This certificate is awarded to

. . . .

for successful completion of

THE FOURTH STEP IN CODING
„BINARY SYSTEM AND CODING"

YOU DID IT

Answer Key

CODE

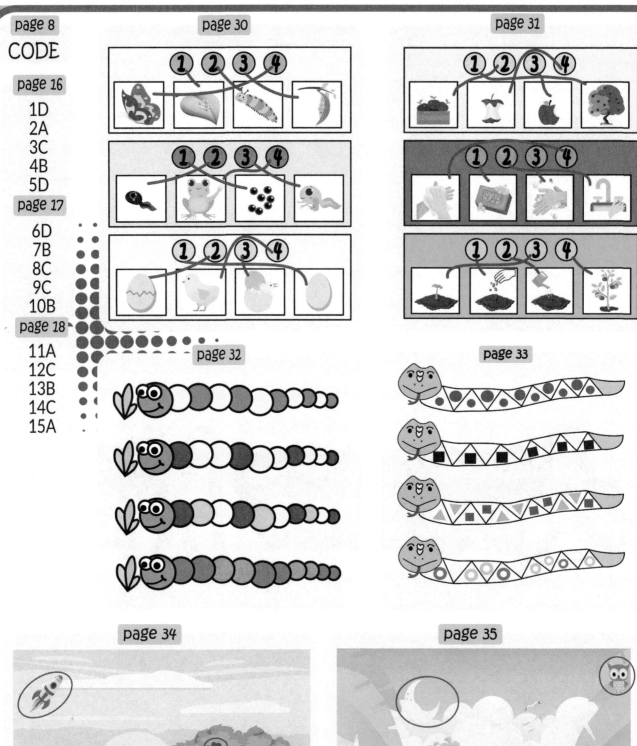

page 30

page 31

page 32

page 33

page 34

page 35

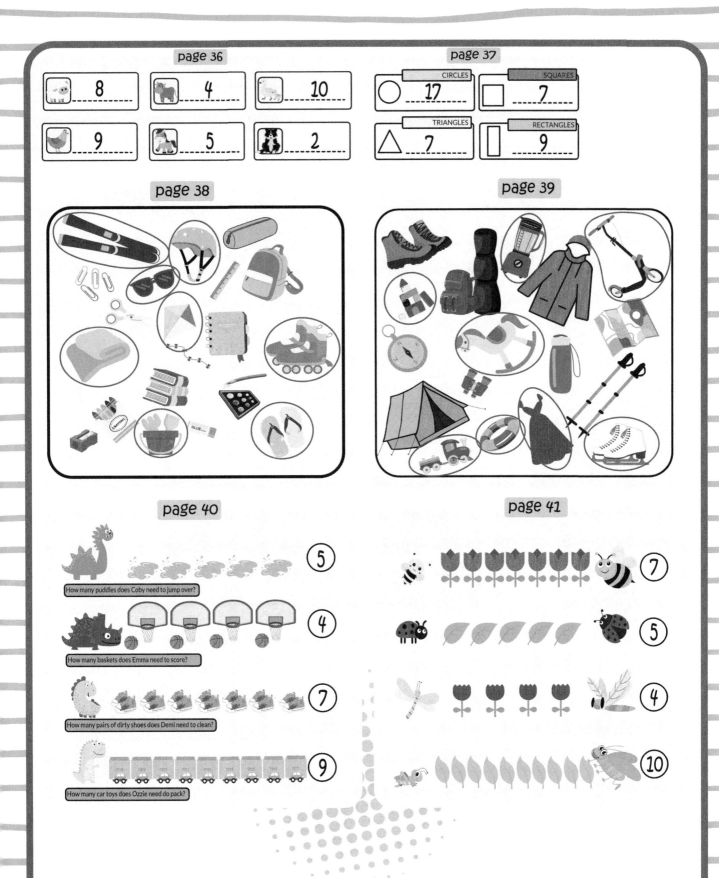

page 36

8
4
10
9
5
2

page 37

CIRCLES 17
SQUARES 7
TRIANGLES 7
RECTANGLES 9

page 38

page 39

page 40

5
How many puddles does Coby need to jump over?

4
How many baskets does Emma need to score?

7
How many pairs of dirty shoes does Demi need to clean?

9
How many car toys does Ozzie need do pack?

page 41

7
5
4
10

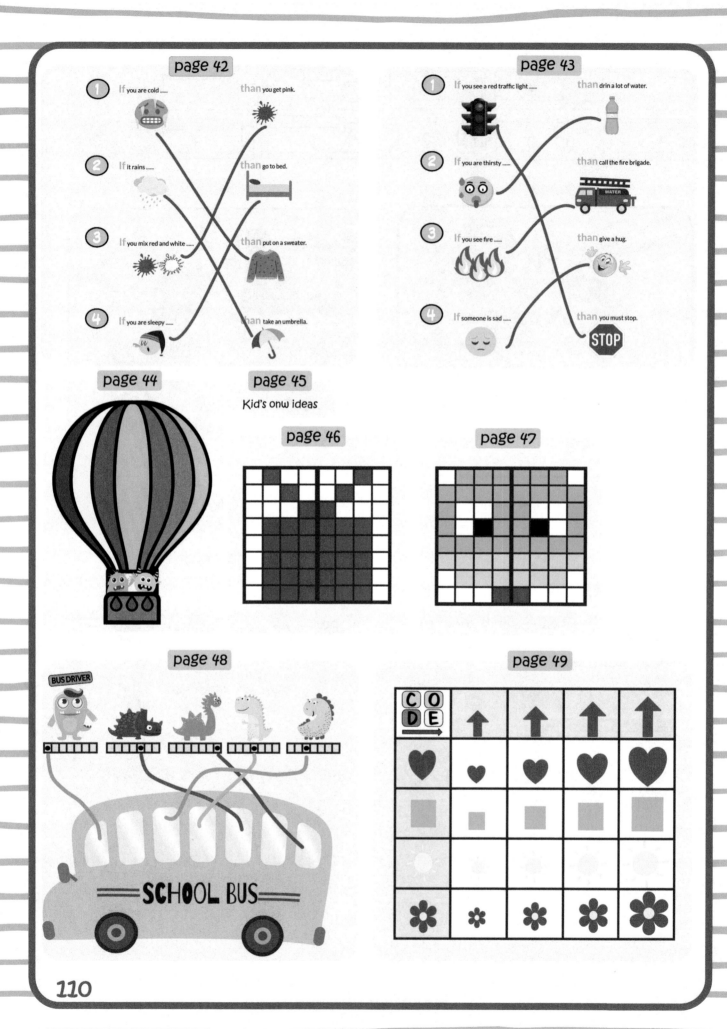

page 42

1. If you are cold ...... / than you get pink.
2. If it rains ...... / than go to bed.
3. If you mix red and white ...... / than put on a sweater.
4. If you are sleepy ...... / than take an umbrella.

page 43

1. If you see a red traffic light ...... / than drin a lot of water.
2. If you are thirsty ...... / than call the fire brigade.
3. If you see fire ...... / than give a hug.
4. If someone is sad ...... / than you must stop.

page 44

page 45

Kid's onw ideas

page 46

page 47

page 48

BUS DRIVER

SCHOOL BUS

page 49

CODE

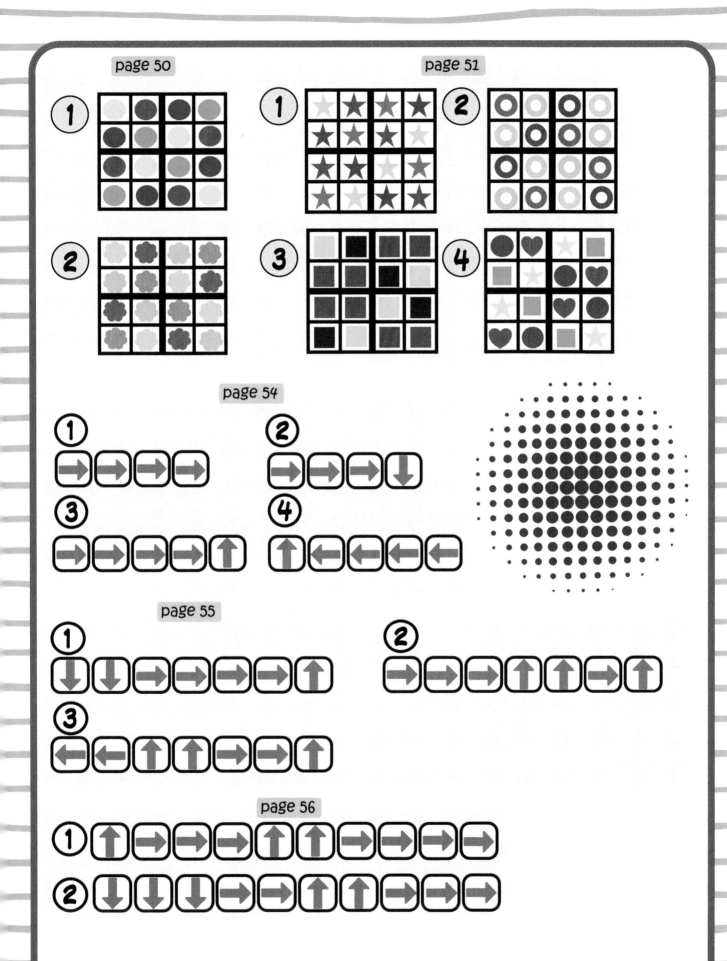

page 50

page 51

page 54

page 55

page 56

page 57

① ↑ ↑ ↑ ← ← ← ↑ ← ←

② ↑ ← ← ↑ ↑ ↑ → → ↓

page 58

① → → ↓ → → ↑ ↑ → → →

② ↓ ↓ ← ← ← ↑ ↑ ← ↓

page 59

① ↑ ↑ → → ↓ → → ↑ ↑ →

② ↑ ↑ ← ← ← ↓ ← ← ↑ ←

page 60

① ↑ ↑ → ↑ ←

② ↓ ↓ → ← ↓

page 61

① ← ← ↑ ↑ → ← ↑ ↑ ← ↓

② ← → ↓ ↓ → ↑ ↓ → ↓ →

page 62	page 63	page 70	page 71	page 72	page 73
① B	① B	① C	① A	① C	① A
② B	② A	② B	② A	② C	② B

page 77

① B
② A
③ A
④ B
⑤ A
⑥ B

page 78

4B
3A
6F
3D

6D
5F
6A
3E

page 79

6B
2D
7G
3F

1G
1C
3B
5E

112

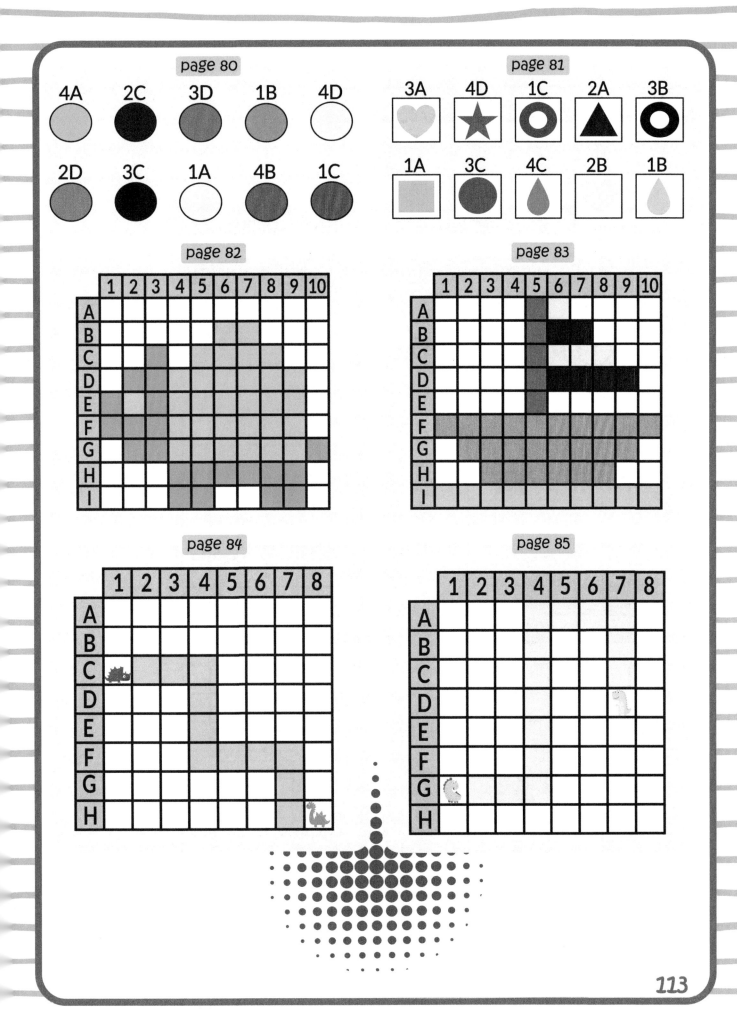

page 80

page 81

page 82

page 83

page 84

page 85

page 86

① 1B 2B 3B 3C 3D 3E 5D 5C

② 1E 1D 1C 1B 2B 2A 3B 4A

page 87

① 1D 2D 3D 4D 4C 4B 4A 5A 6A 7A 7B 6B

② 1B 2A 2B 2C 3C 4C 5C 6C 6D 7D 7C 7B

page 88   page 89

C   **①** A **②** B **③** B

page 98

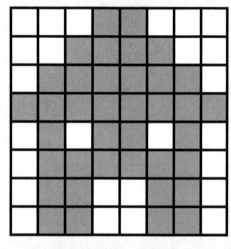

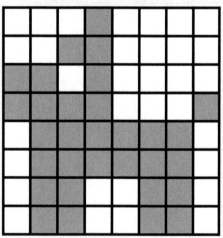

page 99

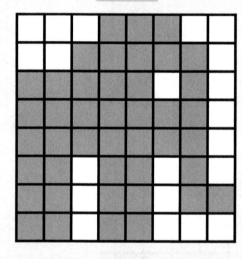

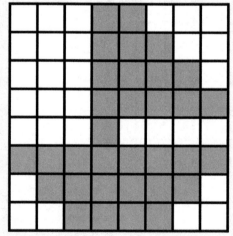

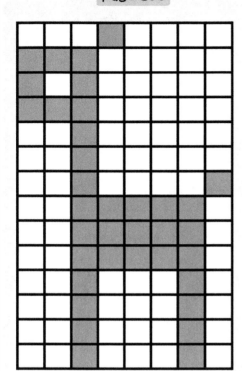

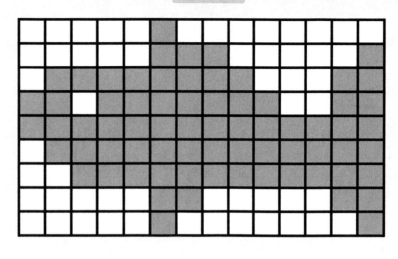

1	1	0	0	0	0	0	0	0
1	1	0	1	1	1	0	0	0
0	1	0	1	0	1	0	0	1
0	1	1	1	0	1	1	1	1

0	0	0	0	0	0	0	1	1
0	1	1	1	1	0	0	1	1
1	1	1	1	1	1	0	1	0
1	1	1	1	1	1	0	1	0
1	1	1	1	1	1	1	1	0
0	1	1	0	0	1	1	0	0

0	0	0	0	0	0	0	0	0
1	1	0	0	0	0	0	1	1
1	1	1	0	1	0	1	1	1
0	1	1	1	1	1	1	1	0
0	0	1	1	1	1	1	0	0
0	1	1	1	1	1	1	1	0
1	1	1	0	1	0	1	1	1
1	1	0	0	1	0	0	1	1
1	0	0	0	0	0	0	0	1

0	0	1	0	0	0	0	0
0	0	1	0	1	0	0	0
0	0	1	1	1	0	0	0
0	0	0	0	0	1	1	1
1	0	0	0	0	1	0	1
1	0	0	0	1	1	1	1
1	1	1	1	1	1	1	0
1	1	1	1	1	1	1	0
1	1	0	0	1	1	0	0
1	0	0	0	0	1	0	0
1	0	0	0	0	1	0	0

CodeBoard to practice :)

IT IS NOT THE END OF OUR ADVENTURE!

WE HAVE GOT A **CODEBOARD** FOR YOU TO PRACTICE CODING!

YOU ONLY NEED TO CUT ALL THE ELEMENTS OUT, FIND A SMALL TOY FOR WHICH YOU WILL MAKE ENDLESS, CREATIVE STEP SEQUENCES USING ARROWS OR COORDINATES TO REACH THE CHOSEN DESTINATION!

THE CODEBOARD CONSISTS OF:

- 1 BOARD (IN TWO PARTS) TO CUT AND GLUE
- 48 ARROW CARDS TO CUT
- 48 OBSTACLES CARDS TO CUT
- 24 DESTINATION CARDS
- 14 LOOP CARDS
- 8 MONSTER CARDS

I WILL EXPLAIN WHAT TO DO WITH THIS CODEBOARD!

This is the CodeBoard.

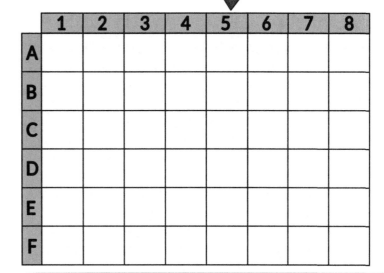

	1	2	3	4	5	6	7	8
A								
B								
C								
D								
E								
F								

These are arrow cards.

These are obstacles cards.

These are destination cards.

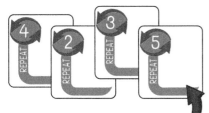

These are loop cards.

These are Dinosaur cards.

Instruction:

Place the Dinosaur Card or a small toy in a chosen square on the CodeBoard.

Place the Destination Card in a chosen square on the CodeBoard.

(Optional) To make your game more difficult put some Obstacles Cards on the board. While going to the destination place the monster or a toy must avoid all the obstacles.

Code the Dinosaur or your toy's way to the destination place using Arrow Cards or writing down on a piece of paper the proper coordinates of the squares.

Important: Do the arrow sequences on the table, not on the board.

Put the CodeBoard and set of cards away when playtime is over!

MY MUM KEEPS SAYING IT!

117

THIS IS MY EXAMPLE:

I HAVE PUT OZZIE CARD ON SQUARE 1D, THE DESTINATION CARD ON 8C. ADDITIONALLY, I HAVE PLACED TWO OBSTACLE CARDS. OZZIE CAN NOT GO THROUGH THE SQUARES WITH OBSTACLE CARDS. BELOW THE CODEBOARD I HAVE CREATED THREE TYPES OF CODES.

	1	2	3	4	5	6	7	8
A								
B								
C							🌿	🏠
D	🦖	🌿						
E								
F								

ARROW CODE: ↑ → → → → → ↓ → → ↑

ARROW CODE WITH LOOPS: ↑ [REPEAT 5 →] ↓ [REPEAT 2 →] ↑

COORDINATE CODE: 1D, 1C, 2C, 3C, 4C, 5C, 6C, 6D, 7D, 8D, 8C.

CODEBOARD (PART I) →

Carefully use the scissors to cut it.
Then, glue it to CodeBoard - Part II.

	1	2	3	4
A				
B				
C				
D				
E				
F				

CODEBOARD (PART II)

Carefully use the scissors to cut it.
Then, glue it to CodeBoard - Part I.

	5	6	7	8

ARROW CARDS

Carefully use the scissors to cut them.

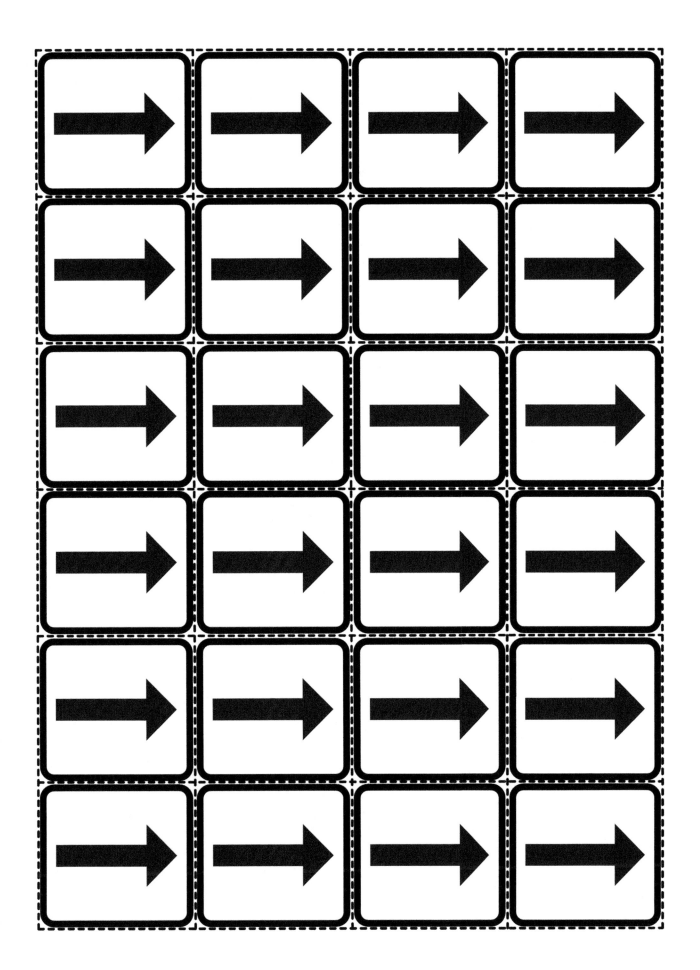

ARROW CARDS

Carefully use the scissors to cut them.

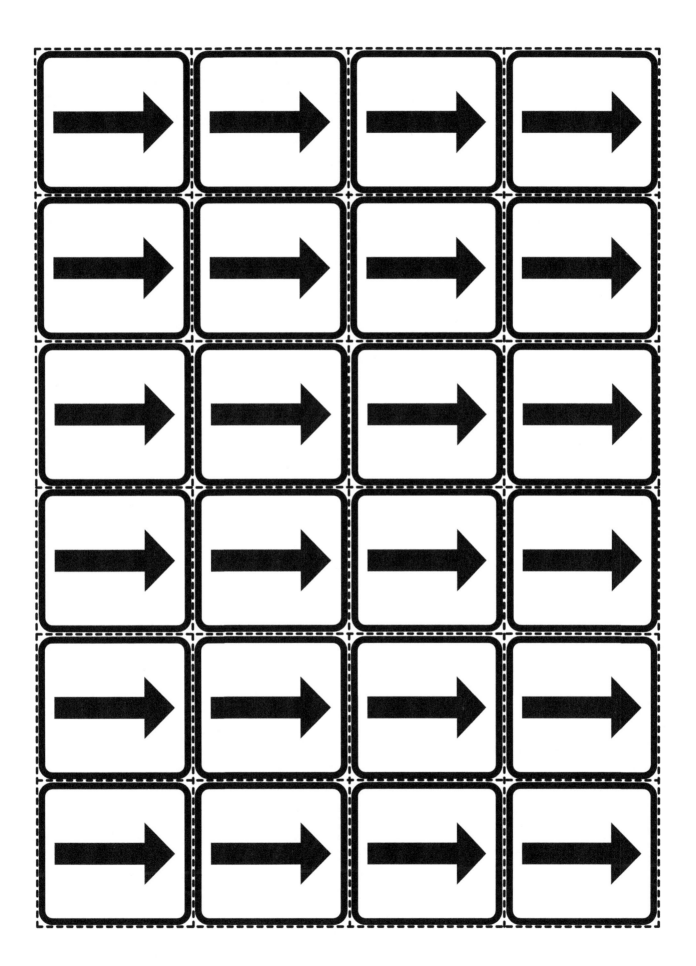

OBSTACLE CARDS

Carefully use the scissors to cut them.

OBSTACLE CARDS

Carefully use the scissors to cut them.

DESTINATION CARDS

Carefully use the scissors to cut them.

LOOP CARDS

Carefully use the scissors to cut them.

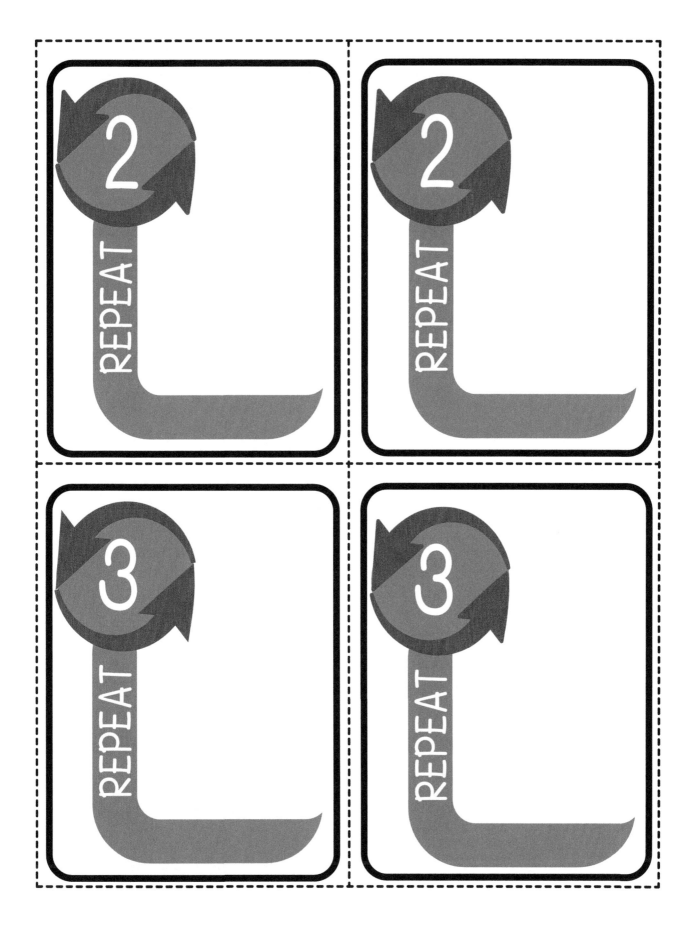

LOOP CARDS

Carefully use the scissors to cut them.

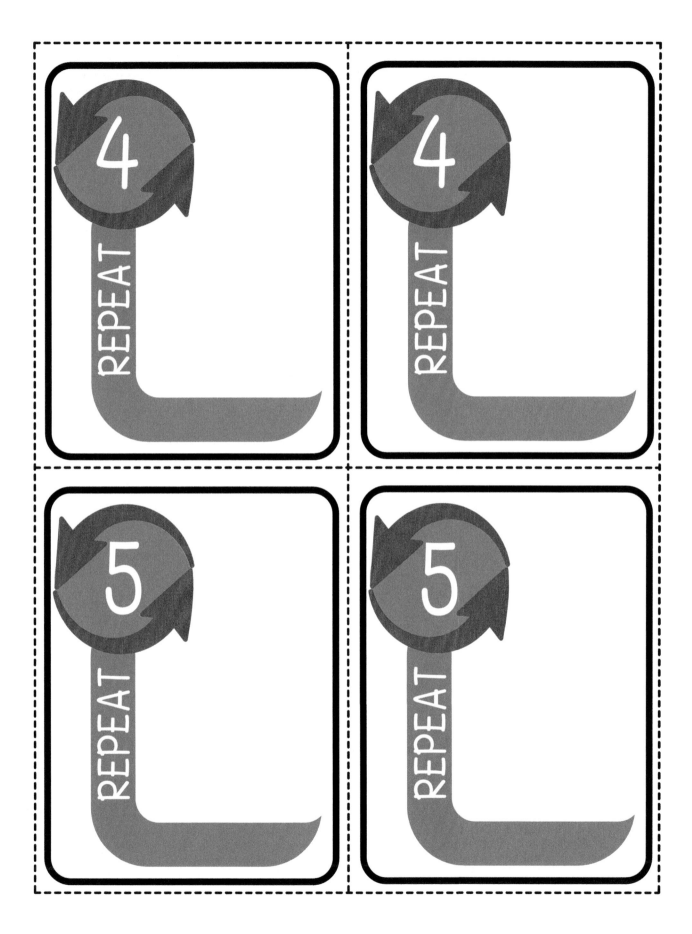

LOOP CARDS

Carefully use the scissors to cut them.

LOOP CARDS

→

Carefully use the scissors to cut them.

DINOSAUR CARDS

→

Carefully use the scissors to cut them.
You can use them instead of
your small toys.

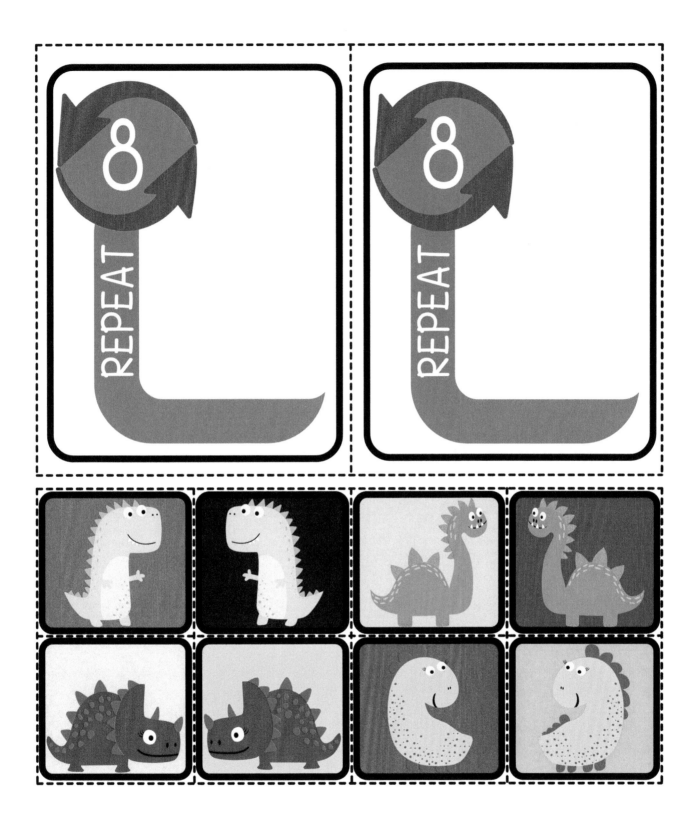

*In the outline draw yourself.

Thank You :)

Julia Dream

Printed in Great Britain
by Amazon

23735717R00079